C000145786

TED MOTT'S
CAMBRIDGE

A Portrait of the City in Old Photographs

by

Michael Rouse

S. B. Publications

For Beryl and Gordon,
who get taken round to see all sorts of odd places.

First published in 1991 by S.B. Publications,
Unit 2, The Old Station Yard, Pipe Gate, Nr. Market Drayton, Shropshire, TF9 4HY.

© Copyright 1991 S.B. Publications

All rights reserved.
No part of the publication may be reproduced, stored in a retrieval system, or
transmitted in any form, or by any means, electronic or mechanical, photocopying,
recording or otherwise, without the prior permission of the publisher.

ISBN 1 870708 76 8

Typeset and printed by Geo. R. Reeve Ltd., Wymondham, Norfolk NR18 0BD.

CONTENTS

CONTENTS

ACKNOWLEDGEMENTS

Especial thanks to Michael Petty and the staff at the Cambridgeshire Collection of the Central Library in Cambridge for all their help and information and to Ed Collinson for printing up the negatives.

My thanks to all those who have provided information, particularly Dr. E.C. Humphries; Carron's Guest House, Cambridge; Don Unwin and those at Hallen's Garage; and John T. Thurston, Senr., who gave me access to G.W. Essex's *The Famous Thurstons* published by the Fairground Society.

Steve Benz for editing and marketing.

INTRODUCTION

Looking through the photographs of the Cambridgeshire Collection in the Central Library in Lion Yard, Cambridge, I kept coming across the work of Ted Mott. The photographs were mainly from the 1920s into the early 1930s and I often thought they would merit a book by themselves.

In 1989 I used some of Ted Mott's photographs in *The Villages of Old Cambridgeshire* and now I am grateful to be able to draw from the whole of his Cambridge negatives in the Cambridgeshire Collection for this volume. With over 1,700 negatives to choose from I have concentrated in this volume on his earlier photographs. Not all the negatives are printed up and where I could, I chose negatives to be printed specially for this selection, although some of the photographs will inevitably have appeared elsewhere.

The early Cambridge photographs are mainly of the old Chesterton area and the river, but there is a fascinating 'bus ride through the town and several other areas. He seems to have avoided the Colleges, perhaps because other photographers were covering these.

It is easy to forget today when we use a light, modern camera, perhaps with a cassette producing thirty-six photographs just how difficult photography was in the 1920s. Ted Mott's equipment was heavy and cumbersome. He had not got the speed of shutter to capture fast movement and he was limited in the number of exposures he could take as he was using glass plates. Add to that the fact that he was probably travelling by bicycle, so life was difficult.

I have visited the scene of nearly every photograph and in some cases taken my own for reference. Had I had to set up a heavy half-plate camera on a tripod for some shots I would never have survived to see the prints, for there is barely time to step out and take a quick snap between the traffic. While many of his views, the shops, public houses are still recognisable, time and again it is the impact of the motor car that is the significant modern factor.

Michael Petty and the staff at the Cambridgeshire Collection have been as helpful as ever, but it is surprising how little anyone knows about Ted Mott. Ted Mott was born in Markyate in Hertfordshire. One odd negative in the collection is of a cluttered general stores with the name E. Mott. I have been told that his family kept a shop in that village. He began his early photography there. The earliest local photographs are taken in the Shelford area in about 1917, but I have been unable to establish if he was living there or why he was there. Dr. E.C. Humphries who went to live in Scotland Road, Chesterton in 1929, remembers Ted Mott and his wife living with, he believes, relatives in Scotland Road at that time. "When I first knew him he was photographing local views but his hands had been poisoned by developer and they were in a terrible state. Because of this he had difficulty in printing the captions on his negatives and we were able to help him a little with this."

Some time in the early 1930s he moved to 144 Shelford Road, Trumpington and from about 1936 to 1947 he and his wife kept a small, cluttered fancy goods shop in Woollards Lane, Great Shelford. He is still remembered as a stockist for Dinky toys and the agent for Hornby model railways. He appears to have died in about 1947 and Dr. Humphries remembers: "a kindly, trusting man who made a meagre living at photography". I would love to find out more and fill in some of the gaps.

Michael Rouse

By the same author in this series:
The Villages of Old Cambridgeshire – A Portrait in Old Photographs and Picture Postcards (1989).

THE TED MOTT NEGATIVE COLLECTION

The catalogue of negatives in the Cambridgeshire Collection refers to some 1,750 photographs. It is in two parts with the prefixes MN and MNH, standing for Mott Negatives and Mott Negatives Humphries. The late Mr. Ken Humphries was the brother of Dr. E.C. Humphries referred to in the introduction. Ken Humphries became friendly with Ted Mott when his family moved to Scotland Road and he remained in contact with him until Ted Mott's death. At that time he then acquired many of his boxes of negatives. He was then instrumental in identifying the rest in a King's Street antiques shop in Cambridge and the Cambridgeshire Collection was able to buy them.

Since the boxes of plates had obviously been split up it is possible that there are other negatives around or that have been lost. This might explain some of the apparent time and number gaps in the collection. All known negatives, however, are now in the Cambridgeshire Collection. The negatives are classified as they were found in various packets and boxes: MN 1 – 108 and MNH 1 – 66. A few are dated and some have been numbered for publication as postcards. The early numbered cards are mainly of Shelford views and are in the 7,000s and 8,000s. They date from 1917 going through to 1921 with some 9,000s around 1921 and 1922. Although there are negatives from the mid 1920s the numbering system is not used. The numbering begins again at the 11,000s with photographs of Newnham, Chesterton, Trumpington and Milton. These appear to date from 1929 to about 1932.

Local titles published in the series: "A Portrait in Old Picture Postcards"

Peterborough, Vols. 1, 2 & 3
The Soke of Peterborough
Wicken – a fen village
The villages of Old Cambridgeshire

Huntingdonshire, Vols. 1 & 2

Hertfordshire, Vols. 1, 2 and 3

Enfield
From Highgate to Hornsey
The Parish of St. Mary, Islington
Islington and Clerkenwell

Brighton and Hove, Vol. 1
Eastbourne, Vols. 1 & 2
Seaford and District, Vols. 1 & 2

Norwich, Vols. 1, 2 & 3
The Norfolk Broads
Holt and District
Melton Constable and District
Swaffham to Fakenham
Great Yarmouth, Vol. 1
West Norfolk
Norfolk's Railways, Vol. 1; G.E.R.
Norfolk's Railways, Vol. 2; M.&G.N.

Beccles and Bungay
East Suffolk
Lowestoft, Vol. 1
West Suffolk Villages

Newcastle-upon-Tyne, Vols. 1 & 2
Old Jarrow

General Titles:
Cats
Aviation: Balloons and Airships
Boys of the Brigade, Vol. 1
Constabulary Duties: A History of Policing
Farming Times: A Chronicle of Farming
The Magic of Multiples: Twins and Triplets

Other titles available and in preparation. For full details write (enclosing S.A.E.) to:
S.B. Publications, Unit 2, The Old Station Yard, Pipe Gate, Market Drayton, Shropshire, TF9 4HY.

Ditton Plough From River.

(MN48/6 1920)

June 1920 and it's May Week. It's fascinating to find some of the earliest negatives in the collection devoted to this great Cambridge tradition. Town and gown gathering together to enjoy a sporting and social occasion. Ditton Paddocks was a popular viewing point. The Rector at Fen Ditton put up marquees, which can be seen on the next two photographs, and sold teas. That well-known riverside public house The Plough also did a brisk business.

(MN48/3 1920)

The inter-College May boat races, which are traditionally held in June, are bumping races. The boats are started in order of a league table or ladder. If the pursuing boat catches the one in front a 'bump' is recorded and the boats change place on the table. The 'Mays' began in 1826 and in Victorian and Edwardian times they attracted huge crowds.

Christ 1 Bumping Jesus 2.

(MN48/2 1920)

There is still a strong Edwardian feel to these photographs, with time seeming to stand still for tradition. However, that great watershed of history, the First World War, has been ended two years and a new age has certainly dawned. It was always difficult for photographers at this time to capture action without blurring the image. Here Ted Mott has tilted his camera and the photograph does give some feel of the race as Christ's No. 1 boat records a bump over Jesus' 2.

'Countess of Bury' House Boat
At Ditton Corner

(MN48/1 1920)

One more from this charming record of the Mays of 1920. This shows the Viscountess Bury pleasure cruiser which Banham's Boats operated on the Cam from 1911. In recent years the Viscountess Bury, splendidly refitted, has been moored at Ely making pleasure cruises on the Ouse.

Station Road Cambridge.

(MNH6/5 1922)

The summer of 1922 and five views taken in the Hills Road and Cherry Hinton Road area of the town. By today's standards this view of Station Road is remarkable for the absence of traffic. In the distance can be seen Rattee and Kett's building and the newly dedicated war memorial.

Hills Road, Cambridge.

(MNH6/9 1922)

It may well have been the recently dedicated war memorial that brought Ted Mott to take this set of photographs. The fine monument depicting a young soldier, helmet in hand and rifle over his shoulder, wearing the laurel wreath of victory was unveiled by the Duke of York on the 3rd of July 1922. It stands on Hills Road looking along Station Road at a point that many young soldiers must have passed as they went to the station.

(MNH6/6 1922)

There are views of Hills Avenue, Cavendish Avenue, Baldock Way and this one of Blinco Grove, which connects Hills Road with Cherry Hinton Road. As the houses show, this was another area of Cambridge which saw development in the late Victorian and Edwardian times. St. John's Church which stands on the corner was dedicated in 1896 and the St. John's parish was included in the Borough of Cambridge in 1912.

(MNH6/12 1922)

Baldock Way off Blinco Grove and obviously new housing on what was the edge of Cambridge. The road appears to end at open fields and that, with the new fencing and recently planted trees, gives the whole street an unlived in appearance.

EB-3838

Cherryhinton Rd. Cambridge.

(MNH6/10 1922)

From the same set of plates but a much livelier street scene of Cherry Hinton Road looking towards Rock Road. The fine group of shops, most with splendid gas globes outside, include Harry Marslen's confectioners and tobacconists; W.R. Fletcher (later Eastman's butchers); James Waugh, grocers, and Harry Davis, bootmaker. Now the same range has a Chinese takeaway, Alric Lighting, Dewhurst Butchers, and Barkers, carpets and vinyl flooring.

(MNH6/11 1922)

This photograph was taken within a few minutes of the previous one. Time taken to set up and record the other side of the street with Onyett's shop in the foreground. The same two men are still talking over the bicycle at the pavement's edge.

(MN96/9 c. 1922)

On another occasion Ted Mott took this very evocative study of H.H. Onyett's, drapers and milliners, at 91 Cherry Hinton Road. Henry Herbert Onyett, the proud owner, could well be standing outside the shop with his staff. The building is unchanged today except it is now occupied by Hair & Co. The tennis courts to the rear have gone though and a veterinary practice is now operating from there.

(MNH46/7 1923)

The same road from a different box of negatives. This time the camera is pointing towards the Cattle Market and Hills Road. Onyett's is directly to the right. William Taylor Archer had the chemist's shop in the foreground, while next to him was Harry Shadbolt's grocers. Again the shopfronts have changed little over the seventy years except today they are Bain Clarkson's Insurance Brokers. The houses beyond though have all lost their iron railings doubtless in the cause of King and Country between 1939 and 1945.

(MNH46/5 1923)

Probably taken on the same visit to the Hills Road area this view of the war memorial shows, on closer inspection, a flock of sheep being driven along the road, presumably coming from the cattle market.

13

(MNH12/15 1922)

Another selection of views from the same box, dated 1922. Perhaps it is the problem of movement causing blurring on the time exposed plates that led so many of the early photographers to record near empty street scenes. Here are two classic examples of Cambridge's tree lined-suburbia.

(MNH12/11 1922)

There is a vehicle parked in the distance, but apart from that there appears to be little difficulty to stand in the middle of the road and record a very quiet scene.

Entrance to Botanic Gardens, Cambridge.

(MNH12/4 1922)

The life and charm that the couple feeding the ducks, with the boy watching, bring to this photograph transforms it totally and makes it one of my particular favourites of these early views.

A Glimpse of St. Peter's Terrace Cambridge.

(MNH12/16 1922)

The cart being pushed along the Trumpington Road adds some life to this otherwise rather ordinary view. It is not much easier today to get more than a glimpse of the substantial Victorian St. Peter's Terrace. Like the similar Scrope Terrace nearby it is set back from the Trumpington Road and screened by mature trees. St. Peter's Terrace took its name from the College on whose land it was built while Scrope commemorates Lady Anne Scrope who gave that parcel of land to Gonville College in 1501.

Trumpington Street, Cambridge

(MNH12/9 1922)

This view is taken from almost the same position as the previous one with St. Peter's Terrace on the left and looking towards the city centre. In the foreground can be seen Misses Sarah and Amelia Harris' shop selling teas, ices and refreshments. In the distance can just be seen the outpatients entrance to Addenbrooke's Hospital.

(MNH 12 /5 1922)

A bequest from Dr. John Addenbrooke who died in 1719 lead to Addenbrooke's Hospital being built on the Trumpington Road in 1740 for the care of 'poor people of any parish or county'. In fact it didn't open until 1766 because of legal and financial problems. The open collonades clearly shown here were enclosed in 1938. When the hospital outgrew this site, it began the move to the new site in Hills Road in May 1962. The old hospital finally closed in 1984 and now the building is being converted for university use.

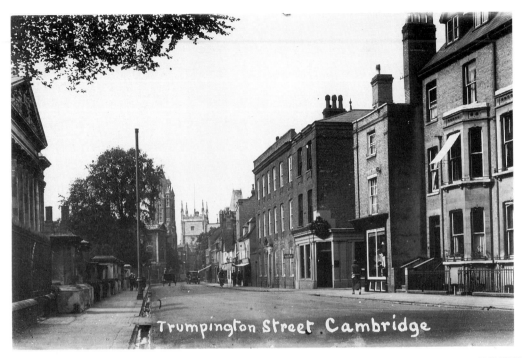

Trumpington Street Cambridge

(MNH12/8 1922)

Trumpington Street again but further towards the centre of town. This view just shows on the left the famous classical front of the internationally renowned Fitzwilliam Museum designed by Basevi and built from the bequest of Richard Viscount Fitzwilliam who died in 1816. The museum was some twelve years in the building after work began in 1837. On the corner of Fitzwilliam Street opposite is G.H. Peck's, chemist's shop, which was established in 1851 shortly after the Fitzwilliam would have opened.

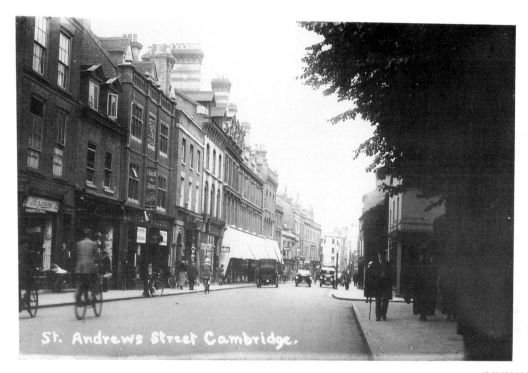

(MNH12/1 1922)

The last of this particular group is one of Ted Mott's rare photographic excursions towards the centre of Cambridge. He is looking towards the city centre and Emmanuel Street junction can be seen on the right. Among the shops on the left are: Flack and Judge's, grocers and Johnson Brothers, with its 'Dyers' sign jutting out over the pavement before the long canopied expanse of Robert Sayle's store which began in St. Andrew's Street in 1840 and is still there today.

(MN 25/3)

An undated odd negative in the collection showing Ye Old Castel Hotel in St. Andrew's Street. This must be from the mid 1920s because the hotel burnt down in 1927. Ye Old Castel stood almost opposite the New Theatre and there is a poster for the theatre prominently displayed announcing 'Sidney Firman's London Radio Dance Band'. The Castle public house was built on part of the site and later a cinema on the rest of the site in 1937.

(MNH 14/2)

Another undated odd negative this time showing Clark's Motor Cycle agent at 7 Northampton Street. These premises were originally the Bell Inn and Northampton Street was formerly known as Bell Lane. The photograph would appear to date from about 1927 and gives a view into the old inn's courtyard.

Northampton Street Corner, Cambridge.

(MNH 8/8)

We can stay in this area of Cambridge for four further views from a different box, again undated but appearing to be mid 1920s and summer time. Three of the same crossroads show the same policeman on traffic duty. Firstly looking towards Chesterton Lane. The attractive range of buildings on the right was renovated by Magdalene College in 1966.

Castle Street, Cambridge.

(MNH 8/1)

This shot is from Magdalene Street looking towards Castle Hill. Ye Olde White Horse became the Cambridge and County Folk Museum in 1934. One of the billboards outside Clark's newsagents is advertising news of 'Cambridge Summer Term'. Frank Webster, whose shop can be seen in the foreground was a baker and confectioner.

(MNH 8/5)

An unusual view from the grounds of St. Giles' Church. An Ortona 'bus can be clearly seen going up Chesterton Lane with the conductor collecting fares on the open upper deck.

The Backs, Cambridge.

(MNH 8/3)

From the same box of negatives an attempt to capture some of the timeless charm of The Backs. King's College Bridge can just be seen as can the pinnacles of King's College Chapel. Although all the trees are not fully in leaf, the number of trees always made this a difficult view to capture.

Jesus Locks, Cambridge.

(MNH 42/15 c. 1928)

Around 1928 Ted Mott took a series of river photographs. The first of these selected from the same box shows the footbridge at Jesus Green. This is the one built in 1892 which replaced an earlier bridge which was at a low level over the sluice and at a high level over the locks. Until ten years or so before this photograph the Cam was still quite a busy commercial river.

(MNH 42/7 c. 1928)

For many years a string of ferries connected Chesterton with Cambridge. In 1889 the River Cam Bridges Act laid down minimum standards for future bridges and the next year John Webster's Victoria Road bridge was built carrying all the A10 traffic through the city. To celebrate the bridge's centenary in 1990 extensive repair work began.

(MNH 42/3 c. 1928)

Another view of John Webster's fine bridge, this time showing Banham's Boatyard through the arch.

(MNH 42/4 c. 1928)

Looking back at the ·Victoria Bridge from the new vantage point of the Fort St. George Bridge. H.C. Banham's Boatyard can now be seen on the right. Banham's owned a number of riverside sites and provided boathouses in Victorian times for a number of Colleges. George Winter was another well known boatyard owner.

(MNH 42/2 c. 1928)

This is the Fort St. George Footbridge between Pretoria Road and Midsummer Common which was opened on 2nd September 1927. The Fort St. George public house, which was built in the sixteenth century during the Seven Years War and named after the Fort St. George in India, originally stood on an island in the Cam. Here was an old river crossing point. The Pauley family operated the ferry until the new footbridge. Their ferry sank shortly before the bridge opened.

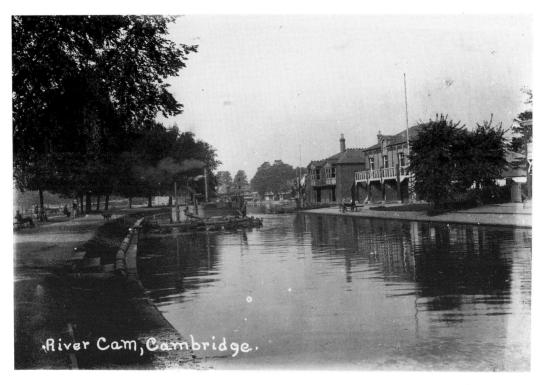

River Cam, Cambridge.

(MNH 42/12 c. 1928)

An interesting photograph as it shows a dredger working almost opposite the Goldie boathouse. The Cam flooded its banks on many occasions, so in 1923 dredging began and continued until 1933. It is recorded that enough silt was removed to cover Parker's Piece to a depth of six feet.

River Cam, Cambridge.

(MNH 42/5 c. 1928)

The Cutter Bridge provided another link for the residents of the rapidly developing Chesterton area with the centre of Cambridge. The bridge soon became known as the Pye Bridge as it provided the main route for workers at the Pye Factory.

(MN 63/11 c. 1928)

The next sequence of photographs continue the journey along the Cam. This one gives a much closer view of the dredger at work.

Cutter Bridge Cambridge

(MN 63/13 c. 1928)

Another view of the Cutter or Pye Bridge and showing Dant's ferry. The Dant family operated the ferry at this point for some sixty years. Cutter Ferry Lane ran down to the ferry, hence the name of the bridge. The same view taken today would show the Elizabeth Way bridge in the background.

Cutler Bridge, Cambri...

(MN63/8 c. 1928)

A different view of the new bridge. It may well have been the opening of these two new footbridges that spurred Ted Mott to take some of these photographs, because he has certainly used both of them in these views and other views of the river.

River Cam, Cambridge.

(MN 63/9 c. 1928)

A lovely photograph showing what was, when erected in 1927, the largest gas holder in East Anglia. Alongside it is the chimney of the Cheddars Lane pumping station. In 1968 a new riverside sewage pumping station was opened and the old works are now the Museum of Technology.

(MN 63/3 c. 1928)

The next easy point of access to the river for the photographer was at Chesterton, so he has moved to just outside the Green Dragon public house in Water Street. The ferries operated to and from the Green Dragon to Stourbridge Common. There were two ferries and this is the smaller ferry for pedestrians with its ferryman, Alf Ford. Stourbridge Common was the site of the main Cambridge Fair held in the second half of September and the early part of October.

Horse Grind Ferry Chesterton, Cambridge

(MN63/4 c. 1928)

The larger Horse Grind Ferry seen here could carry a horse and cart across the river. Both ferries ceased operating in 1935 when a new footbridge was constructed at this point. 1935 was the last year of the old Stourbridge Fair which had gradually dwindled in size and importance.

Near Horse Grind Ferry Chesterton, Cambridge

(MN 63/2 c. 1928)

This pleasant study taken from the same group of negatives as the previous two photographs appears to have been taken with the camera set up on the Horse Grind Ferry.

(MN 63/16 c. 1928)

Ferries were often operated by or in conjunction with public houses and this is the Pike and Eel Ferry at Chesterton, a little way downstream from the Horse Grind. The added interest in these photographs is that it is the time of the May Races again about eight years after the first photographs of the Mays seen at the start of this book.

Pike & Eel Ferry, Chesterton, Cambridge.

(MN 63/14 c. 1928)

Good crowds line the banks with people using every vantage point, these photographs capture the atmosphere of the occasion. The interesting figure with the baskets in the left foreground looks as if he has just come from the Pike and Eel, where licensee, Arthur Brown, would be enjoying considerable trade. Both photographs clearly show the chain on the larger ferry used to draw it across the river, but also on the smaller punt nearer the camera.

River Cam, C......... .....y Week.
Waiting For The Boa...

(MN 63/15 c. 1928)

"Waiting for the Boats" and the last from this particular group of negatives probably dating from the summer of 1928. The camera has been set up on the same point of the tow path for all three photographs and in this one Ted Mott has turned to look downstream. Crowds line the tow path and the Stourbridge Common side as far as the camera can see.

Chesterton Fair was also known as the "Bumps Fair" and was held in June at the time of the Mays. It was held in a field down the Fen Road adjacent to the towpath. Fairs in the Cambridgeshire area are synonymous with the Thurston family. At this time William Thurston was the owner and riding master of the Electric Gondolas seen here. William was the son of Henry Thurston who was born in Cambridge in 1847 and began the "Famous Thurstons" family of showmen.

(MN 17/2)

These Three Abreast Gallopers built by Savages of King's Lynn were bought by Henry Thurston in 1901 and a considerable advance on the small hand-operated children's roundabout that he had begun touring fêtes with, some thirty years before. These gallopers were operated by Royal Command at a Buckingham Palace Garden Party.

(MN 17/9)

A group of what may be fairground workers was not the usual sort of photograph taken by Ted Mott. They are standing in front of the Foster No. 12415 Dreadnought traction engine bought in 1909 to drive the Three Abreast Gallopers. These negatives are undated but may have been taken at the same time as the previous photographs near the Pike and Eel.

(MN 10/3 1926)

The Tivoli cinema on Chesterton Road opened on 19th March 1925. The architect was George P. Banyard. A Colleen Moore film "The Desert Flower" released in 1925 is being advertised. The Tivoli Café is next door and the corner of the café can just be seen near The Spring public house. The Tivoli closed on 19th November 1956 and after a period as a warehouse is now The Exchange restaurant and health club, while The Spring, after a period known as The Rob Roy, is now The Boatrace.

(MN 10/2 1926)

Showing part of Chesterton Road from around the area known at the time as Mitcham's Corner. This corner of Chesterton Road and Victoria Avenue took its popular name from the large department store shown here. Since the opening of the Victoria Bridge in 1890 this junction was a focal point in many journeys, but as motor traffic increased it became, in time, an extremely busy and congested corner.

(MN 10/1 1926)

This range of shops near Mitcham's Corner helped to cater for the growth of Cambridge on the Chesterton side of the river, particularly after the new bridge. There is the Chesterton Road Post Office with W.J. Oxberry's stationer's shop; next to that is C.T. Green's confectioner's and dairy shop; then the projecting front of Freeman Hardy and Willis.

(MN 10/8 1926)

The same range of shops photographed at a later date; Oxberry's and Green's have added new shop fronts with projecting bay windows at first-floor level to bring them into line with Freeman Hardy and Willis. A new post box has also been placed at the pavement's edge.

(MN 89/3)

Frederick Cousins was an entrepreneurial grocer who established his business at the corner of Cam and Montague Roads in 1922. Cam Road was a quiet cul-de-sac leading down to the river and at first sight a strange choice of location. However, just across the road was the huge Pye factory, one of Cambridge's major employers, and many of the workers would come past the shop making their way into the town. These premises in time became Cambridge's first delicatessen – Joseph's Continental Stores – patronised by the factory workers. For some twenty years, however, this has been a guest house now known as "Carrons".

Fleur De Lys Hotel, Chesterton.

(MNH 2/9)

A little further along Cam Road on the corner with Humberstone Road, the Fleur de Lys would have also benefitted from having Pye's factory just across the road. The Fleur de Lys has not changed much today except the corner door has gone. What has changed, however, is the whole area.

(MN 47/3 c. 1928)

In 1971 after years of debate and finally compulsory purchase Cam Road became part of Queen Elizabeth Way leading to the new bridge. Montague Road and Humberstone Road were blocked off at that point and the new road was given over to Cambridge's enormous volume of traffic. This photograph showing part of Chesterton Hall and a quiet leafy road is unrecognisable today as is the Old Chesterton Road, now blocked off just before the corner of Cam Road. Just beyond the Hall today is the huge Chesterton Road – Elizabeth Way roundabout.

(MN 47/8 c. 1928)

A selection of Chesterton photographs (pages 55–67) taken from around 1928 when Ted Mott was living in Scotland Road. This one shows the Post Office at 50 High Street. Frank Arthur Bailey kept the shop and post office at this time. The post office, now enlarged, still occupies the same building in what is a relatively unchanged terrace. The next terrace, however, has been replaced by modern housing.

(MN 47/18 c. 1928)

The Ortona 'bus waits at the terminus. In the background with the distinctive upper storey is The Wheatsheaf public house. The Wheatsheaf was demolished some time in the mid 1950s as Hallen's garage wth its motor showroom and motor cycle department extended. The adjoining house was also demolished and the attractive house with the porch, the only surviving building in the view is now the accounts department of Hallen's.

(78/30/14A)

This photograph is from a negative not in the collection. The different angle gives a view of the old almshouses which stood on the corner of Union Lane. The side and sign of The Haymakers public house can just be seen on the left. After a period of dereliction the almshouses were demolished in the early 1950s and the site incorporated into Hallen's.

(MN 47/2 c. 1928)

The Premier Dance Hall in Union Lane, still fondly remembered by many as the place where they met their match. In 1936 the late Leslie W. Hallen bought the hall and began his motor business there. In fact the roof line of the former building can be clearly seen above the modern showroom. This was the start of the business which now dominates both sides of the Union Lane junction with the High Street.

(MN 47/10 c. 1928)

Chesterton has changed considerably since these photographs were taken. This view of the corner of Church Street taken from the High Street is unrecognisable today as all the cottages on the corner have gone and been replaced by modern housing. The roof with its tall chimney stacks and the old wall and gate of No. 22 Church Street can be seen in the centre of the view.

(MN 47/12 c. 1928)

The Dog and Pheasant at 115 High Street, Chesterton, seen over sixty years ago. While the hoardings beyond it were all replaced by housing soon after this photograph was taken, the public house is still instantly recognisable and in business today. The sign advertises "Lacon's Yarmouth Beers" which were brewed at the Albion Brewery in Coronation Street in Cambridge.

(MN 47/1 c. 1928)

Two more views from the same set as Ted Mott moved down the High Street. The Dog and Pheasant is now behind him on his left and part of the hoarding can still be seen. Many of the buildings have survived and are identifiable. There is still a shop on the corner of Thrifts Lane and the roof of what was the Wesleyan Chapel dating from 1858 can be seen in the distance.

(MN 47/9 c. 1928)

Looking back along the street with Radford's wet fish and chip shop in the foreground. The previous photograph may well have included Mr. Radford and his son outside their shop. They had not been in business there long and later the shop became the Co-op Fish and Chip shop. In more recent years it was John Powley's television shop and is currently a dentist's. The cottages next to it have gone and Grayling Close has been built. The white building on the corner is the former Red Bull public house.

(MN 64/1 1927)

Eastman's butchers were at no. 66 High Street; at the time of this photograph F. Hastead was the manager. Nothing remains of the old building.

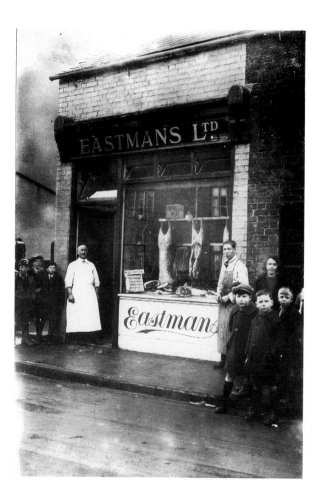

(MN 47/4 c. 1928)

A view from near the Indian Chief public house to the almshouses on the corner of Union Lane. Despite the substantial appearance of many of these buildings nothing has survived. The fragment of poster on the wall says "Vote for Mrs. McNair". It must have been effective for Marjorie McNair was an elected representative for the East Chesterton ward for the Borough Council.

(MN 47/15 c. 1928)

An informal group of pupils outside the St. Andrew's Church of England school which stood at the bottom of the High Street. The school closed in 1981 and the building was demolished with the site redeveloped for housing.

(MN 47/16 c. 1928)

A charming, and now lost, view of the historic riverside hostelry The Green Dragon at Chesterton. The two ferries can be seen; the Horse Grind loaded with a horse and cart. Alf Ford was the ferryman here for many years until the footbridge was built in 1935. The footbridge over the Cam at this point and some residential building close to the site of the smaller ferry have now obscured this once open view from Stourbridge Common.

water St., Chesterton Cambridge

(MN 75/4 c. 1928)

A closer view of The Green Dragon, belonging to Panton Street brewer, Bailey and Tebbutt. Greene King acquired B. & T. and still have The Green Dragon as one of their houses. Changes to the sign board and exterior painting show this photograph was probably taken a year or so from the previous one.

Bus Terminus, Chesterton, Cambridge

(MN 9/2 c. 1926/7)

In about 1926 or 27 Ted Mott took a series of photographs from the open top deck of this Ortona 'bus on its scheduled route – Service 1 – from Chesterton through the city to the railway station. Photograph No. 56 gives another view of the 'bus terminus at the junction of the High Street and Chapel Lane. The Co-op in the background was built on the site of The Old Bleeding Heart, once the home of Charles Rowell the world champion long distance 'go-as-you-please' runner, who in 1879 ran 500 miles in six days at Madison Square Gardens, New York.

(MN 9/8 c. 1926/7)

Chesterton Road going past Jesus Green and the locks with Strange's boat yard on the right. From his position at the front of the 'bus he took some shots while on the outward journey and some on the return. This was on the return journey but I have organised the sequence to follow the route.

(MN 9/3 1926/7)

Magdalene College on the left and the splendid medieval to late 18th-century buildings on the west side of the street. At the time of this 'bus ride these buildings were under threat of demolition. The College had commissioned Edwin Lutyens to design Benson Court. This would have doubled the width of the street. Work began in 1932 when the west range was built on Fisher Lane, near the Bin Brook, but then funds ran out and Magdalene Street survived.

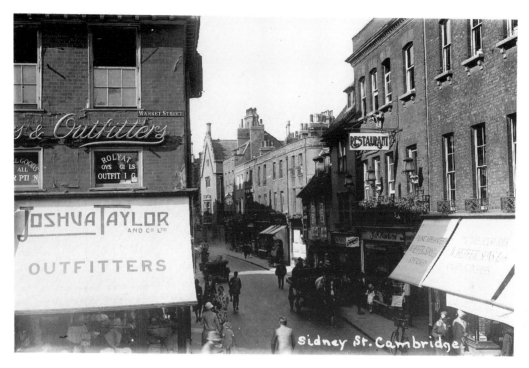

(MN 9/5 c. 1926/7)

Ted Mott rarely took his camera into the centre of Cambridge. Three famous Cambridge retail names are picked out from his vantage point. The first is Joshua Taylor's who have closed this year. They moved from Ely in 1860 and acquired this corner site in 1900. The second is W. Heffer & Sons stationery shop and next to them G.P. Hawkins and their famous Dorothy restaurant, a popular meeting place for eating and dancing.

(MN 9/7 c. 1926/7)

The already busy junction of Sidney Street with St. Andrew's Street, Hobson Street and Petty Cury. Here stood the Barnwell Gate built by Henry III in the thirteenth century. The gate of Christ's College dominates the middle of the view. The entrance to the bustling Petty Cury was to the right of the 'bus.

(MN 9/4 c. 1926/7)

A very solid policeman on traffic duty at the junction of Regent Street with Lensfield Road, Gonville Place and Hills Road. 'Saints Garage, Open Day & Night' can be clearly seen beyond the advertising hoarding at what today is a much changed corner. Regent Street, on the direct route to and from the railway station and the town centre, has always been a busy street.

(MN 9/6 c. 1926/7)

Hills Road, just over Hyde Park Corner heading towards the railway station with the Perse School on the left behind the railings.

(MN 9/1 c. 1926/7)

A view looking along Hills Road taken on the return journey, as were several of the photographs. The spire of the Roman Catholic Church built in 1890 can be seen ahead. The Globe Hotel can be seen on the right and behind it the tower of St. Paul's church. Unfortunately this fascinating series of views does not include one of the railway station. Some photographs were lost because of the blurring caused by the movement of the 'bus or other traffic, but for some sixty five years ago and using the equipment he did it was a remarkable effort.

Perse School, Cambridge.

(MN 7/4 c. 1928)

Another box of views keeps us in the Hills Road area. These could date from about 1928. The Perse School is a public school founded by Stephen Perse, M.D. under his will in 1625. The boys' school moved from Free School Lane to this site on the corner of Hills Road and Gonville Place in 1890. In 1959 the Perse boys' moved to a new site further along Hills Road.

(MNH 7/9 c. 1928)

A good view of the Hills Road Methodist Church on the corner of Norwich Street. The church was demolished in 1973. The lamps in the foreground above the lorry are for the Dorset Temperance Hotel's garage. The tall building with the flagpole was the House of Commons public house.

(MNH 7/7 c. 1928)

The coming of the railway and the opening of the station in 1845 brought great expansion to the eastern side of the city. Hills Road developed as an important thoroughfare. New churches like the Roman Catholic and the Wesleyan Chapel, which was built in 1870, helped to meet the needs of the growing city.

(MNH 7/3 c. 1927)

St. Paul's Church on Hills Road was built as the centre of a new parish created in 1845.

(MNH 7/8 c. 1928)

The final photograph in this particular section returns to the war memorial and apart from the blur of some bicycles, carts and a 'bus in the distance, traffic is light. The distinctive premises of that most distinguished stonemasons, Rattee and Kett, can be seen on Station Road.

(MNH 5/3 c. 1926)

James Walford Berry's Ortona 'Bus Company was the first successful operator in the city. It began in 1907, and in February 1914 the horse-drawn tram service stopped running. Rival 'bus companies like the Whippet in 1919 and Burwell and District in 1922 resulted in the need for a central 'bus terminus. Despite strong opposition the Drummer Street 'bus station was opened in 1925.

(MN 11/1 1926)

By the 1920s residential Cambridge was spreading further out with various housing schemes to the north of the city. This photograph dated 1926 shows new shops being built on the Milton Road to cater for this expansion. These are now numbered 109–111 Milton Road, today a newsagents and a carpet shop.

(MN 11/3 1926)

Photographed nearby, probably on the same visit, is an established small store. This is E. Songer's with its fascinating array of advertising signs. Today Alan Bedford, florists, occupies 139 and 141 Milton Road, the business incorporating the cottage next door.

Ramsden Square, Cambridge.

(MNH 18/2 c. 1927)

Two photographs from 1927 showing the expansion of Cambridge in the Milton Road area. Ramsden Square winds round from Milton Road to Kings Hedges Road. It has all the appearance of a corporation housing scheme built on a very open site. By a strange coincidence the young trees shown in 1927 having reached a gnarled maturity, Ramsden Square today has just been planted with another batch of saplings.

HOUSES IN COURSE OF ERECTION MILTON Rd. CAMBRIDGE 1927

(MNH 18/8 1927)

The expansion of Cambridge in late Victorian times with areas like the De Freville estate, new Chesterton and Newnham provided mainly middle class villas. The poorer families complained of their 'appalling living conditions'. These 1927 houses being built along Milton Road were offered for sale by the Council for £579, with £5 down and weekly payments of £1.05.

(MNH 30/18 1920)

Two almost timeless images of Cambridge. In fact they are dated 1920 and quite early photographs in the collection. The River Cam or Granta has always been a major feature of Cambridge life, whether it is for the May Races, punting or simply paddling along on a summer's day. In the middle of the photograph can be seen the Sheep's Green Swimming Station where the legendary Charles Driver was custodian, swimming coach and life saver from 1903 to 1937.

(MNH 32/8 1920)

Between Cambridge and Grantchester, 1920.

(MN 108/28)

Amongst all the negatives are two shopfronts, one photographed in 1911 at the time of the Coronation of George V and this one. On closer inspection they are the same shop. It is not in Cambridge and it is not in Great Shelford. Is it therefore Ted Mott's shop in Markyate? Dr. Humphries informed me that someone remembered when Ted Mott had a shop there – "a shop that sold so many things that it was difficult to find anything". Funnily enough I have heard the same description used about the shop in Great Shelford. I would love to know more.